PRINCEWILL LAGANG

The Venture Capital Handbook for Entrepreneurs

First published by PRINCEWILL LAGANG 2023

Copyright © 2023 by Princewill Lagang

All rights reserved. No part of this publication may be reproduced, stored or transmitted in any form or by any means, electronic, mechanical, photocopying, recording, scanning, or otherwise without written permission from the publisher. It is illegal to copy this book, post it to a website, or distribute it by any other means without permission.

Princewill Lagang asserts the moral right to be identified as the author of this work.

First edition

*This book was professionally typeset on Reedsy.
Find out more at reedsy.com*

Contents

1	Introduction to Venture Capital	1
2	Preparing for Venture Capital Success	5
3	Finding the Right Investors	9
4	Navigating Due Diligence	14
5	Negotiating Venture Capital Terms	18
6	Scaling Your Venture with Venture Capital	23
7	Managing the Investor Relationship	27
8	Navigating Common Challenges in Venture-Backed Startups	31
9	Achieving Significant Milestones and Scaling Your Startup	35
10	Navigating Successful Exits	39
11	The Entrepreneur's Next Chapter	43
12	The Ever-Evolving Entrepreneurial Landscape	46
13	Summary	49

1

Introduction to Venture Capital

Title: "The Venture Capital Handbook for Entrepreneurs"

In the fast-paced world of entrepreneurship, access to capital is often the lifeblood of innovation and growth. For many startups and early-stage companies, securing the necessary funding to turn their ideas into reality can be a daunting and challenging task. This is where venture capital plays a pivotal role, providing not only financial support but also strategic guidance to promising startups. This chapter serves as your introduction to the world of venture capital, setting the stage for the invaluable insights and guidance you'll find in this handbook.

1.1 Defining Venture Capital

Venture capital, often abbreviated as VC, is a type of private equity investment that is focused on providing financing to startups and small businesses with high growth potential. Unlike traditional loans or bank financing, venture capital involves equity investment, where investors receive ownership stakes in exchange for their funding. This partnership model aligns the interests of entrepreneurs and investors, as both stand to gain from the company's success.

1.2 The Role of Venture Capitalists

Venture capitalists (VCs) are the individuals or firms responsible for providing the funding. These investors, often seasoned professionals, bring not only financial resources but also a wealth of experience and industry connections. They act as mentors and advisors to the entrepreneurs, offering strategic guidance, helping with business development, and assisting in critical decision-making.

1.3 The Startup Landscape

Startups are companies in their early stages, typically in search of funding to scale their operations. They are known for their innovation, agility, and disruptive potential. Many startups operate in technology-driven industries, such as software development, biotech, artificial intelligence, or e-commerce, but the venture capital model extends to a wide range of sectors.

1.4 The Venture Capital Lifecycle

Understanding the venture capital lifecycle is essential for entrepreneurs seeking VC funding. This process typically includes the following stages:

1.4.1 Pre-Seed Stage
- Idea and concept development
- Proof of concept
- Building a founding team

1.4.2 Seed Stage
- Product development
- Initial market validation
- Early customer acquisition

1.4.3 Early-Stage (Series A and B)
  - Scaling operations
  - Expanding market reach
  - Building a sustainable business model

1.4.4 Late-Stage (Series C and beyond)
  - Preparing for exit strategies (IPO, acquisition)
  - Further scaling and international expansion

1.5 The Pitch and Due Diligence

For entrepreneurs seeking venture capital, a well-crafted pitch is essential. VCs review numerous business proposals and select only a small percentage for investment. Your pitch should clearly articulate your business idea, its unique value proposition, the market opportunity, and your team's capability to execute the plan.

Due diligence is the process by which VCs assess the potential risks and rewards of an investment. They will scrutinize your business model, market research, financial projections, legal structure, and more. It's crucial to be prepared for this rigorous examination.

1.6 The Venture Capital Ecosystem

Venture capital is just one piece of the broader entrepreneurial ecosystem. Other key players include angel investors, incubators, accelerators, and corporate venture capital arms. Understanding how these components interact can help you make informed decisions about your funding strategy.

1.7 Your Venture Capital Journey

As you embark on your venture capital journey, it's important to recognize that securing funding is not the end goal. It's a means to an end—a tool to help you achieve your long-term vision. In the chapters that follow, we'll delve into the specifics of the venture capital process, from finding the right investors to negotiating terms and managing the partnership effectively.

This handbook is your comprehensive guide to navigate the intricate world of venture capital successfully. Whether you're a first-time entrepreneur seeking seed funding or a seasoned business leader looking to scale your company, the insights and strategies within these pages will equip you with the knowledge and confidence to make the most of your venture capital experience. In the next chapter, we'll explore the foundational steps to prepare for your venture capital journey.

2

Preparing for Venture Capital Success

In the entrepreneurial world, success often begins with thorough preparation. Before you dive headfirst into the venture capital landscape, it's essential to lay the groundwork for your journey. This chapter will guide you through the crucial steps and considerations to ensure you're well-prepared to seek venture capital funding and build a solid foundation for your startup.

2.1 Refining Your Business Idea

2.1.1 Idea Validation
   - Start by validating your business concept. Is there a real need for your product or service? Are customers willing to pay for it? Conduct market research, surveys, and interviews to gather data that supports your idea.

2.1.2 Problem-Solution Fit
   - Ensure your solution effectively addresses a significant problem in the market. Fine-tune your value proposition to resonate with your target audience.

2.1.3 Competitive Landscape

- Understand your competition. Who are your direct and indirect competitors? What differentiates your offering? You'll need a compelling story about how you plan to outperform the competition.

2.2 Building a Strong Team

2.2.1 Co-Founders and Key Roles

- Assemble a skilled and diverse founding team. Identify co-founders with complementary skill sets. Define key roles and responsibilities to cover all aspects of your business.

2.2.2 Advisors and Mentors

- Seek out experienced advisors and mentors who can provide guidance and industry insights. A well-rounded advisory board can significantly enhance your credibility with potential investors.

2.3 Creating a Solid Business Plan

2.3.1 Executive Summary

- Craft a compelling executive summary that provides a concise overview of your business. Highlight your unique selling points and the problem you're solving.

2.3.2 Business Model

- Clearly define your business model, including revenue streams, pricing strategy, and customer acquisition channels.

2.3.3 Financial Projections

- Develop detailed financial projections, including income statements, balance sheets, and cash flow forecasts. Investors will want to see how you plan to use their funds and achieve profitability.

2.3.4 Go-to-Market Strategy

- Lay out your marketing and sales strategy. How will you reach and acquire customers? What is your customer acquisition cost?

2.4 Legal and Intellectual Property Considerations

2.4.1 Legal Structure

- Choose an appropriate legal structure for your business (e.g., LLC, C-Corp, S-Corp). Consult with legal experts to ensure compliance with regulations.

2.4.2 Intellectual Property

- Protect your intellectual property, including patents, trademarks, copyrights, and trade secrets. This can be a critical asset that adds value to your startup.

2.5 Product Development and Prototyping

2.5.1 Minimum Viable Product (MVP)

- Develop a minimum viable product to demonstrate your concept's feasibility. This can be an essential tool for showcasing your idea to investors.

2.5.2 Prototyping

- Create prototypes or mockups to visualize your product or service. This can help potential investors better understand your vision.

2.6 Financial Preparedness

2.6.1 Bootstrapping

- Consider bootstrapping your startup with your savings or revenue before seeking venture capital. A solid financial foundation can make your business more attractive to investors.

2.6.2 Funding Needs

- Calculate your funding needs. How much capital do you require to achieve your milestones? Be clear about how you plan to allocate the investment.

2.6.3 Valuation
- Understand your startup's valuation and be prepared to justify it. Valuation is a crucial factor in determining how much equity you'll need to give up in exchange for funding.

2.7 Pitch Deck and Presentation

2.7.1 Pitch Deck
- Create a compelling pitch deck that effectively communicates your business idea, market opportunity, team, and financial projections. Your pitch deck is often your first impression on potential investors.

2.7.2 Presentation Skills
- Hone your presentation skills. Confidence and clarity in your pitch can make a significant difference in investor meetings.

By thoroughly preparing your startup in these areas, you'll be in a strong position to attract venture capital funding. In the chapters that follow, we will explore the next steps in your venture capital journey, from identifying the right investors to navigating the due diligence process and negotiating terms. Stay focused, and remember that preparation is key to venture capital success.

3

Finding the Right Investors

Securing venture capital for your startup is a significant milestone, and one of the most critical aspects of this journey is finding the right investors who align with your vision and goals. In this chapter, we will explore the process of identifying and connecting with potential investors who are the best fit for your startup.

3.1 Defining Your Investment Needs

Before you start your search for investors, it's crucial to have a clear understanding of your funding requirements. Consider the following factors:

3.1.1 Funding Round
  - Determine which stage of funding you are currently seeking (seed, Series A, Series B, etc.). Different investors specialize in different stages.

3.1.2 Funding Amount
  - Calculate the exact amount of capital you need. Be specific about how you plan to allocate these funds.

3.1.3 Milestones

- Define the milestones you aim to achieve with the investment. Having a clear plan for what you'll do with the funds will instill confidence in potential investors.

3.2 Identifying the Right Investors

3.2.1 Angel Investors

- Angel investors are typically individuals who provide early-stage funding. They often have a strong network and industry expertise.

3.2.2 Venture Capital Firms

- Venture capital firms are professional investment organizations that manage funds from various sources. They invest in startups at different stages.

3.2.3 Corporate Venture Capital (CVC)

- Some established companies have their own venture arms (CVC). Partnering with these entities can provide not only funding but also strategic opportunities.

3.2.4 Online Platforms and Networks

- Consider using online platforms like AngelList or Crunchbase to identify potential investors. Attend startup events and networking functions to make connections.

3.2.5 Geography

- Pay attention to the geographical preferences of investors. Some investors prefer to invest in specific regions or industries.

3.2.6 Industry Focus

- Look for investors with a history of investing in your industry. They are more likely to understand your market and value proposition.

3.3 Creating a Target Investor List

3.3.1 Research
- Conduct thorough research on potential investors. Understand their investment history, portfolio companies, and investment criteria.

3.3.2 Qualify Potential Investors
- Assess whether potential investors are a good fit for your startup based on your funding needs and their investment preferences.

3.3.3 Build Relationships
- Establish relationships with potential investors. Attend industry events, reach out through introductions, and participate in pitch events.

3.3.4 Warm Introductions
- A warm introduction from someone in your network can significantly increase your chances of securing a meeting with an investor.

3.4 Crafting Your Pitch

3.4.1 Elevator Pitch
- Develop a concise elevator pitch that summarizes your startup's value proposition, mission, and what you're looking for from investors.

3.4.2 Pitch Deck
- Create a compelling pitch deck that provides a detailed overview of your business, market opportunity, team, financials, and milestones.

3.5 Reaching Out to Investors

3.5.1 Email Outreach
- Craft personalized emails to investors, clearly expressing your interest in connecting. Highlight what makes your startup attractive.

3.5.2 Warm Introductions

- Leverage your network to secure warm introductions to potential investors. Mutual connections can vouch for your credibility.

3.5.3 Networking Events

- Attend startup and venture capital events where you can meet investors in person. These events provide an opportunity to make a memorable impression.

3.6 Navigating the Initial Meetings

3.6.1 Due Diligence

- Be prepared to answer questions and provide additional information during initial meetings. Investors will want to understand your business in more detail.

3.6.2 Investor Fit

- Assess whether the investor is a good fit for your startup. Consider not only their financial offer but also their strategic value and alignment with your goals.

3.7 Decision-Making and Negotiations

3.7.1 Term Sheets

- If an investor is interested, they may present a term sheet outlining the proposed terms and conditions of the investment. Seek legal advice to understand the implications.

3.7.2 Negotiation

- Be prepared for negotiations. You and the investor may need to find common ground on issues such as valuation, equity, and governance.

Finding the right investors is a crucial step in your venture capital journey.

The next chapter will explore the due diligence process and what you can expect as investors evaluate your startup in detail. Remember, building the right investor relationships can set your startup on a path to success.

4

Navigating Due Diligence

As you progress in your venture capital journey and secure the interest of potential investors, you'll encounter a critical phase: due diligence. This chapter delves into the due diligence process, providing insights into what investors will examine, how to prepare, and what to expect during this thorough evaluation of your startup.

4.1 Understanding Due Diligence

4.1.1 What is Due Diligence?
 - Due diligence is the comprehensive examination of your startup's financial, legal, operational, and strategic aspects by potential investors. It helps them assess the risks and opportunities associated with the investment.

4.1.2 Why is Due Diligence Important?
 - Investors conduct due diligence to minimize risks and ensure that the information provided in your pitch is accurate. A successful due diligence process builds trust and confidence.

4.2 Due Diligence Categories

4.2.1 Financial Due Diligence
- Investors will scrutinize your financial records, including income statements, balance sheets, cash flow statements, and revenue projections.

4.2.2 Legal Due Diligence
- Legal experts will examine your contracts, agreements, intellectual property, compliance with regulations, and any outstanding legal issues.

4.2.3 Operational Due Diligence
- Investors will assess your day-to-day operations, scalability, technology infrastructure, and production processes.

4.2.4 Market Due Diligence
- This involves evaluating the market opportunity, competitive landscape, customer behavior, and your go-to-market strategy.

4.2.5 Management Team Due Diligence
- Investors will evaluate your team's skills, experience, and the roles of key team members.

4.3 Preparing for Due Diligence

4.3.1 Organize Your Documents
- Have all relevant documents, records, and agreements readily accessible. This includes financial statements, contracts, and corporate governance documents.

4.3.2 Legal and Compliance
- Ensure that your startup is compliant with all applicable laws and regulations. Address any legal issues or concerns proactively.

4.3.3 Intellectual Property
- Protect your intellectual property with patents, trademarks, and copy-

rights. Be ready to demonstrate the value of your IP portfolio.

4.3.4 Financial Records
- Keep your financial records accurate and up-to-date. Any discrepancies or inaccuracies can erode investor confidence.

4.3.5 Operational Documentation
- Document your operational processes, technology stack, and business operations. Clarity in these areas is critical.

4.3.6 Team Bios
- Prepare detailed bios of your team members, highlighting their qualifications and contributions.

4.4 The Due Diligence Process

4.4.1 Investor Team
- Expect a team of investors, including financial, legal, and operational experts, to conduct the due diligence.

4.4.2 Information Requests
- Investors will request various documents and information about your startup. Be responsive and transparent.

4.4.3 Site Visits
- Investors may visit your offices or production facilities to assess your operational capabilities.

4.4.4 Interviews and Meetings
- Be prepared for interviews with investors and their experts. These meetings may delve into specific aspects of your business.

4.5 Addressing Concerns and Questions

4.5.1 Transparency
- Be transparent about any challenges or concerns that arise during the due diligence process. Honesty is crucial.

4.5.2 Mitigating Risks
- Develop strategies to address potential risks or weaknesses in your startup. Investors will appreciate your proactive approach.

4.5.3 Negotiations
- The due diligence process may lead to negotiations, particularly if concerns or discrepancies emerge.

4.6 Closing the Deal

4.6.1 Final Review
- After due diligence, investors will conduct a final review of their findings.

4.6.2 Investment Decision
- Once satisfied, investors will make a decision on whether to proceed with the investment.

4.6.3 Closing Documents
- If the decision is positive, both parties will work on closing documents and finalizing the investment.

Navigating due diligence can be intense, but it is a necessary step to secure venture capital funding. A well-prepared and transparent approach will build trust with investors and increase the likelihood of a successful outcome. In the next chapter, we'll explore the negotiation process and the key terms to consider in your investment agreement.

5

Negotiating Venture Capital Terms

Negotiating the terms of your venture capital investment is a crucial phase in your journey to securing funding for your startup. In this chapter, we will explore the key components of a venture capital deal, the negotiation process, and the factors to consider when determining the terms of the investment.

5.1 The Term Sheet

5.1.1 Introduction to the Term Sheet
 - The term sheet is a non-binding document that outlines the preliminary terms and conditions of the investment. It serves as a framework for the negotiation process.

5.1.2 Key Elements of a Term Sheet
 - The term sheet typically includes details on the investment amount, valuation, equity ownership, investor rights, governance, and other essential terms.

5.2 Investment Amount and Valuation

5.2.1 Investment Amount

- Negotiate the total amount of capital the investor will provide. Be clear on how you plan to use the funds to achieve your milestones.

5.2.2 Valuation

- Determine the pre-money and post-money valuation of your startup. This will impact the percentage of equity you will offer in exchange for the investment.

5.3 Equity Ownership

5.3.1 Founder Equity

- Discuss the equity ownership structure, considering how much ownership founders and key team members will retain after the investment.

5.3.2 Investor Equity

- Define the equity stake that the investor will receive in exchange for their capital.

5.4 Investor Rights

5.4.1 Board Seats

- Determine the number of board seats that the investor will hold. Consider how this affects your startup's governance.

5.4.2 Protective Provisions

- Define the protective provisions that give the investor a say in specific decisions, such as selling the company or issuing more shares.

5.4.3 Information Rights

- Specify the level of access and information the investor is entitled to regarding your startup's operations and financials.

5.5 Liquidation Preferences

5.5.1 Liquidation Preferences
- Discuss the liquidation preference, which defines the order in which investors and founders are paid in the event of an exit (e.g., acquisition or IPO).

5.6 Dividends and Anti-Dilution

5.6.1 Dividends
- Determine if investors will receive dividends and the conditions under which they will be paid.

5.6.2 Anti-Dilution
- Address anti-dilution provisions to protect the investor's equity in case of future fundraising rounds.

5.7 Exit Strategy

5.7.1 Exit Options
- Discuss the possible exit strategies, such as an initial public offering (IPO), acquisition, or merger, and how the proceeds will be distributed.

5.8 Terms for Conversion and Redemption

5.8.1 Conversion Rights
- Define the conditions under which the investor can convert their preferred shares into common shares.

5.8.2 Redemption Rights
- Address any redemption rights, which allow the investor to require the company to buy back their shares.

5.9 Protective Covenants

5.9.1 Protective Covenants
- Negotiate protective covenants that outline restrictions on the company's actions, such as taking on debt, changing the business's core nature, or acquiring other companies.

5.10 Due Diligence and Conditions

5.10.1 Due Diligence
- Define the timeframe for completing due diligence, and ensure that you meet all the conditions stipulated in the term sheet.

5.11 Closing the Deal

5.11.1 Legal Counsel
- Engage legal counsel to review the final investment documents, ensuring they align with the agreed-upon terms.

5.11.2 Finalizing the Agreement
- Collaborate with the investor's legal team to finalize the investment agreement, which will include a shareholder agreement, subscription agreement, and other relevant documents.

5.11.3 Funding and Share Issuance
- Once the agreement is signed, the investor will transfer the funds, and you will issue the agreed-upon shares.

5.12 Post-Investment Management

5.12.1 Investor Relations
- Maintain a positive and transparent relationship with your investors, keeping them informed about your startup's progress.

5.12.2 Governance

- Ensure the startup's governance reflects the terms agreed upon in the investment agreement, including board seats and protective provisions.

Effective negotiation of venture capital terms is a delicate balance between securing the necessary funding and preserving the long-term health of your startup. Careful consideration of these terms and the guidance of legal experts can help you achieve a mutually beneficial agreement with your investors. In the following chapters, we will explore post-investment strategies, including scaling your business and managing the investor relationship effectively.

6

Scaling Your Venture with Venture Capital

Securing venture capital funding is a significant achievement for your startup, but it's just the beginning of your journey. In this chapter, we will explore how to use your newly acquired capital to scale your business successfully, taking it to the next level of growth and profitability.

6.1 Setting Growth Goals

6.1.1 Define Key Metrics
  - Identify the key performance indicators (KPIs) that align with your business objectives. These might include customer acquisition, revenue growth, user engagement, or market expansion.

6.1.2 Short-Term and Long-Term Goals
  - Establish both short-term and long-term growth goals. Short-term goals might focus on immediate expansion, while long-term goals could involve achieving market leadership.

6.2 Allocating Capital

6.2.1 Budgeting
- Develop a comprehensive budget that outlines how you will allocate the venture capital funds. Prioritize spending in areas that directly contribute to your growth goals.

6.2.2 Hiring and Talent Acquisition
- Consider expanding your team to fill key roles that support your growth strategy, such as sales, marketing, product development, and customer support.

6.2.3 Marketing and Customer Acquisition
- Invest in marketing and customer acquisition strategies to expand your user base or customer list. These strategies can include digital marketing, advertising, and partnerships.

6.2.4 Product Development
- Continue improving and expanding your product or service to meet market demands and maintain a competitive edge.

6.2.5 Scaling Operations
- Evaluate your operational infrastructure and adjust it to accommodate increased demand and a larger customer base.

6.3 Market Expansion

6.3.1 Geographic Expansion
- If your startup has a regional focus, consider expanding into new markets, either nationally or internationally.

6.3.2 Market Segmentation
- Identify niche markets or customer segments that present growth opportunities and tailor your strategies accordingly.

6.4 Customer Retention and Engagement

6.4.1 Customer Support
- Enhance customer support and engagement initiatives to retain existing customers and foster brand loyalty.

6.4.2 Feedback Loops
- Establish feedback mechanisms to gather insights from your customer base, which can inform product development and marketing strategies.

6.5 Strategic Partnerships

6.5.1 Identify Potential Partners
- Seek strategic partnerships with other companies that can help you expand your market reach or enhance your product offerings.

6.5.2 Alliances and Collaborations
- Collaborate with other organizations to share resources and capabilities, such as co-marketing, co-development, or joint ventures.

6.6 Measuring and Adapting

6.6.1 Regular Assessment
- Continuously measure and assess your progress against your growth goals and KPIs. Be prepared to adapt your strategies as needed.

6.6.2 Data-Driven Decision-Making
- Use data and analytics to inform your decisions, optimizing marketing, product development, and operations.

6.7 Risk Management

6.7.1 Identifying Risks

- Be vigilant in identifying potential risks that could hinder your growth. These might include market changes, competition, regulatory issues, or financial challenges.

6.7.2 Mitigation Strategies
- Develop contingency plans and mitigation strategies to address potential risks and ensure the sustainability of your growth efforts.

6.8 Investor Relations

6.8.1 Transparency and Reporting
- Maintain open and transparent communication with your investors. Provide regular updates on your startup's progress and performance.

6.8.2 Investor Involvement
- Engage your investors strategically, leveraging their expertise and networks to support your growth initiatives.

Scaling your venture with venture capital is an exciting and challenging journey. Effective execution of your growth strategies, combined with ongoing measurement and adaptation, will be key to realizing your startup's full potential. In the subsequent chapters, we will explore topics such as managing the investor relationship, achieving milestones, and addressing common challenges in the world of venture-backed startups.

7

Managing the Investor Relationship

Securing venture capital funding is not only about obtaining financial resources but also about building a collaborative and productive relationship with your investors. In this chapter, we will explore how to manage the investor relationship effectively, fostering trust, communication, and alignment with your startup's goals.

7.1 The Importance of Investor Relations

7.1.1 Beyond the Check
 - Understand that investors bring more than capital to the table. They offer experience, expertise, and a valuable network that can accelerate your startup's growth.

7.1.2 Long-Term Partnership
 - Recognize that the investor relationship is a long-term partnership. Building a strong rapport can lead to continued support and additional funding in the future.

7.2 Communication and Transparency

7.2.1 Regular Updates

- Provide regular updates on your startup's progress, achievements, and challenges. This can include monthly or quarterly reports.

7.2.2 Transparent Reporting

- Be transparent about any issues or setbacks. Addressing challenges openly demonstrates your ability to manage them effectively.

7.2.3 Open Dialogue

- Encourage an open and two-way dialogue with your investors. Listen to their feedback and insights, and be receptive to their suggestions.

7.3 Leveraging Investor Expertise

7.3.1 Mentorship and Advice

- Seek mentorship and advice from your investors, especially in areas where they have expertise. Their guidance can be invaluable.

7.3.2 Networking Opportunities

- Utilize your investors' networks and connections to forge partnerships, secure customers, and access additional resources.

7.4 Aligning Interests

7.4.1 Shared Vision

- Ensure that you and your investors share a common vision for the future of the company. Misalignment can lead to conflicts and challenges.

7.4.2 Goal Setting

- Collaborate with your investors to set clear goals and milestones that align with your long-term strategy.

7.5 Resolving Disputes

7.5.1 Conflict Resolution
- Address conflicts or disagreements with a constructive and solution-oriented approach. Escalate disputes only when necessary.

7.5.2 Legal Counsel
- If conflicts become unmanageable, consult with legal counsel to protect the interests of both parties.

7.6 Governance and Board Management

7.6.1 Effective Board Meetings
- Conduct board meetings efficiently, focusing on strategic discussions and decision-making. Ensure that all board members are well-prepared.

7.6.2 Governance Structure
- Maintain a strong governance structure that reflects the terms agreed upon in the investment agreement, including the number of board seats.

7.7 Exit Strategy and Liquidity Events

7.7.1 Alignment on Exit
- Keep investors informed about your exit strategy and any potential liquidity events, such as acquisitions or IPOs.

7.7.2 Exit Timing
- Discuss the timing of exit events and ensure that investors are on board with the chosen strategy.

7.8 Financial Accountability

7.8.1 Responsible Financial Management
- Maintain a high level of financial accountability. Investors expect the efficient use of capital and responsible financial practices.

7.8.2 Financial Reporting
- Provide detailed financial reports that reflect your startup's financial health and performance.

7.9 Investor Updates

7.9.1 Regular Meetings
- Schedule regular meetings or calls with your investors to keep them updated on your progress.

7.9.2 Annual Reports
- Consider providing annual reports that encompass the key highlights of the year and the outlook for the future.

Managing the investor relationship is a continuous process that requires open communication, strategic collaboration, and a commitment to shared success. By actively engaging with your investors and leveraging their expertise, you can maximize the benefits of their involvement in your startup. In the next chapter, we will explore common challenges and potential solutions that venture-backed startups encounter as they strive to grow and succeed.

8

Navigating Common Challenges in Venture-Backed Startups

Venture-backed startups operate in a dynamic and often turbulent environment. In this chapter, we'll explore some of the common challenges that entrepreneurs encounter and provide guidance on how to navigate these hurdles effectively.

8.1 Financial Management and Runway

8.1.1 Burn Rate
- Be vigilant about your burn rate, which represents the rate at which your startup is spending its capital. Careful budgeting can extend your runway and buy you more time to achieve your milestones.

8.1.2 Cash Flow Management
- Keep a close eye on cash flow. Effective management ensures that your startup can cover its operational expenses and meet its financial obligations.

8.2 Market Competition

8.2.1 Competitive Analysis

- Continuously analyze your competitors and adapt your strategies to stay ahead. Understand their strengths and weaknesses and use this knowledge to your advantage.

8.2.2 Differentiation

- Differentiate your product or service from the competition. Focus on delivering unique value to your customers.

8.3 Team Building and Retention

8.3.1 Talent Acquisition

- Attract and retain top talent to drive your startup's growth. An exceptional team is often the key to success.

8.3.2 Culture and Values

- Cultivate a strong company culture and values that resonate with your team. A positive workplace environment can boost morale and productivity.

8.4 Scaling Challenges

8.4.1 Operational Efficiency

- Ensure your startup's operations can scale effectively to accommodate increased demand.

8.4.2 Technology Infrastructure

- Invest in a robust technology infrastructure to support your growth and ensure the scalability of your product or service.

8.5 Regulatory and Compliance Issues

8.5.1 Stay Informed

- Keep abreast of industry regulations and changes in the legal landscape.

Failure to comply with regulations can lead to fines and reputation damage.

8.5.2 Legal Counsel
- Engage legal counsel to navigate complex regulatory issues and ensure your startup is in compliance.

8.6 Customer Acquisition and Retention

8.6.1 Customer Acquisition Costs
- Monitor customer acquisition costs to ensure they are sustainable and aligned with your budget.

8.6.2 Customer Retention Strategies
- Develop strategies to retain existing customers, as it's often more cost-effective than acquiring new ones.

8.7 Product Development Challenges

8.7.1 Prioritization
- Prioritize your product development efforts based on market demand, customer feedback, and your long-term vision.

8.7.2 Iteration and Testing
- Embrace an iterative approach to product development, using feedback and data to refine your offering.

8.8 Intellectual Property Protection

8.8.1 IP Strategy
- Maintain a comprehensive intellectual property strategy to protect your innovations and assets.

8.8.2 Patents and Trademarks

- Continuously assess and enforce your patents and trademarks to safeguard your intellectual property.

8.9 Managing Investor Expectations

8.9.1 Realistic Projections
- Set and communicate realistic expectations with your investors. Overpromising and underdelivering can damage the investor relationship.

8.9.2 Open Dialogue
- Foster an open and constructive dialogue with your investors to address any concerns or issues promptly.

Navigating these challenges is a natural part of the entrepreneurial journey. By addressing them proactively and with a strategic mindset, you can minimize their impact and position your venture-backed startup for long-term success. In the next chapter, we will delve into strategies for achieving significant milestones and scaling your startup to new heights.

9

Achieving Significant Milestones and Scaling Your Startup

Scaling a venture-backed startup involves setting and achieving significant milestones that propel your company to new heights. In this chapter, we will explore strategies for achieving these milestones and scaling your business effectively.

9.1 Defining Significant Milestones

9.1.1 Product Development Milestones
  - Identify key product development goals, such as new features, product enhancements, or platform expansions.

9.1.2 Revenue Targets
  - Set revenue goals that align with your growth trajectory. This might involve increasing sales, upselling existing customers, or diversifying revenue streams.

9.1.3 User Acquisition and Growth

- Define targets for user acquisition and user growth. This could include expanding your customer base, increasing user engagement, or reaching specific market segments.

9.1.4 Market Expansion
- Outline plans for entering new markets, both domestically and internationally, if relevant to your business.

9.1.5 Operational Efficiency
- Streamline operations to achieve cost savings and operational efficiency, allowing you to allocate resources more strategically.

9.2 Allocating Resources

9.2.1 Budget Allocation
- Allocate resources, including capital, talent, and technology, to support the achievement of your milestones.

9.2.2 Talent and Team Growth
- Hire and train the talent needed to meet your growth goals. Build cross-functional teams that can support your scaling efforts.

9.2.3 Technology Infrastructure
- Invest in technology and infrastructure that can handle the increased demands of your growing customer base and expanded operations.

9.2.4 Marketing and Sales Strategies
- Develop and execute marketing and sales strategies that align with your growth goals, ensuring you reach and engage new customers effectively.

9.3 Iterative Improvement

9.3.1 Agile Approach

- Embrace an agile and iterative approach to achieving your milestones. Continuously gather feedback and make adjustments as necessary.

9.3.2 A/B Testing
- Use A/B testing and data analysis to optimize your product, marketing campaigns, and user experience.

9.4 Customer Success and Retention

9.4.1 Customer Support
- Enhance your customer support and success initiatives to ensure that customers are satisfied and engaged.

9.4.2 Customer Feedback
- Leverage customer feedback to refine your product, address pain points, and add value for your customers.

9.5 Partner and Alliances

9.5.1 Strategic Partnerships
- Forge strategic partnerships and alliances with other businesses that can help you reach your milestones, expand your market reach, and share resources.

9.5.2 Co-Marketing and Co-Development
- Collaborate with partners on joint marketing campaigns or co-development projects that can accelerate your growth.

9.6 Data-Driven Decision-Making

9.6.1 Analytics and Reporting
- Use data analytics and reporting tools to measure your progress and assess your performance against your milestones.

9.6.2 Key Performance Indicators (KPIs)
- Define and track KPIs that are directly related to your growth goals and provide insights into your success.

9.7 Scaling Challenges

9.7.1 Scalability
- Continuously assess the scalability of your operations, technology, and infrastructure as you achieve your milestones.

9.7.2 Team Alignment
- Ensure that your team is aligned with the scaling strategies and is prepared to take on the challenges and opportunities that come with growth.

9.8 Investor Engagement

9.8.1 Investor Updates
- Keep your investors informed about your progress and milestone achievements. Highlight how their support has contributed to your success.

9.8.2 Leverage Investor Networks
- Tap into your investors' networks and connections to facilitate partnerships, customer introductions, or further funding.

Achieving significant milestones is a testament to your startup's growth and potential. By setting clear goals, allocating resources effectively, and employing iterative strategies, you can scale your venture-backed startup to new heights. In the next chapter, we will explore the nuances of successful exits, whether through an acquisition or an initial public offering (IPO).

10

Navigating Successful Exits

Exiting a venture-backed startup can be a momentous event, and the route you choose, whether through acquisition or an initial public offering (IPO), has significant implications for you and your investors. In this chapter, we will delve into the intricacies of successful exits and the factors to consider when approaching this critical decision.

10.1 The Exit Decision

10.1.1 Timing
- Determine the right timing for your exit. It can be influenced by various factors, including market conditions, your startup's growth, and investor expectations.

10.1.2 Alignment
- Ensure that the chosen exit strategy aligns with your long-term goals and those of your investors.

10.2 Acquisition as an Exit Strategy

10.2.1 Pros of Acquisition

- Explore the advantages of an acquisition, such as a quicker liquidity event, the potential to retain a role in the company, and the opportunity to benefit from synergies with the acquiring company.

10.2.2 Identifying Acquirers

- Identify potential acquirers who align with your startup's vision and are willing to offer a competitive valuation.

10.2.3 Negotiating the Deal

- Engage in negotiations to secure favorable terms, both financially and with regard to post-acquisition roles and responsibilities.

10.3 Initial Public Offering (IPO) as an Exit Strategy

10.3.1 Advantages of an IPO

- Consider the benefits of going public, such as access to a larger pool of capital, increased visibility, and the ability to offer liquidity to your existing investors.

10.3.2 IPO Preparation

- Prepare your startup for an IPO by ensuring financial transparency, strong corporate governance, and compliance with regulatory requirements.

10.3.3 IPO Process

- Engage with underwriters and legal advisors to navigate the IPO process, from registration with regulatory authorities to the issuance of shares.

10.4 Due Diligence and Disclosure

10.4.1 Thorough Due Diligence

- Prepare for an extensive due diligence process, providing comprehensive information and documentation to the acquiring company or regulatory authorities.

10.4.2 Regulatory Compliance

- Ensure that your startup complies with all legal and regulatory requirements, addressing any issues before they become obstacles to your exit.

10.5 Post-Exit Considerations

10.5.1 Integration (for Acquisition)

- Successfully integrate your startup into the acquiring company, harmonizing operations, culture, and team structures.

10.5.2 Post-IPO Operations

- After an IPO, continue managing your company's operations and performance to meet the expectations of public shareholders.

10.6 Investor Relations Post-Exit

10.6.1 Communication

- Maintain open communication with your investors post-exit, addressing their concerns and providing updates on the performance of the company.

10.6.2 Financial Reporting

- Continue to provide financial reports and statements, adhering to the standards of transparency expected by investors and regulators.

10.7 Evaluating Success

10.7.1 Measuring Success

- Assess the success of your exit strategy by comparing it to the goals and expectations you set at the beginning of your venture.

10.7.2 Lessons Learned

- Reflect on the lessons learned throughout your entrepreneurial journey and the exit process, incorporating them into your future endeavors.

Exiting a venture-backed startup represents the culmination of your hard work and the realization of your startup's potential. By making informed decisions and engaging with the process strategically, you can maximize the benefits of your exit and move on to new opportunities and challenges with valuable experience and insights.

11

The Entrepreneur's Next Chapter

With the successful exit of your venture-backed startup, you've reached a significant milestone in your entrepreneurial journey. Now, it's time to explore the possibilities and consider what your next chapter may hold. In this chapter, we will examine various paths and opportunities for entrepreneurs after exiting their startups.

11.1 Reflecting on Your Journey

11.1.1 Celebrate Achievements
- Take the time to celebrate your achievements and acknowledge the hard work, dedication, and persistence that brought you to this point.

11.1.2 Lessons Learned
- Reflect on the lessons learned, both from your startup's successes and challenges. These experiences will be invaluable in your future endeavors.

11.2 Opportunities for Entrepreneurs

11.2.1 Serial Entrepreneurship

- Consider starting a new venture. Serial entrepreneurship is a path taken by many successful entrepreneurs who are eager to tackle new challenges.

11.2.2 Angel Investing
- Use your knowledge and capital to become an angel investor, supporting other startups and emerging entrepreneurs.

11.2.3 Venture Capital
- If you have a passion for the venture capital ecosystem, consider joining a venture capital firm or launching your own.

11.2.4 Advisory and Consulting
- Share your expertise by offering advisory services or consulting to startups and businesses seeking guidance.

11.2.5 Philanthropy and Social Impact
- Explore opportunities to make a positive impact by engaging in philanthropy, supporting charitable causes, or launching social impact initiatives.

11.2.6 Education and Mentorship
- Give back to the entrepreneurial community by becoming a mentor or educator, helping the next generation of entrepreneurs succeed.

11.3 Balancing Personal and Professional Goals

11.3.1 Work-Life Balance
- Achieving a balance between your personal and professional life is essential for your well-being and long-term success.

11.3.2 Personal Growth
- Focus on personal growth and self-discovery as you transition into new ventures and opportunities.

11.4 Embracing Change

11.4.1 Embrace Change
- Embrace the changes and challenges that come with the transition. Adaptability and resilience will be your greatest assets.

11.4.2 Staying Informed
- Stay informed about market trends, emerging technologies, and evolving opportunities to remain relevant in your new ventures.

11.5 The Next Chapter's Impact

11.5.1 Defining Success
- Define your own version of success for the next chapter, and be prepared to measure your progress and achievements accordingly.

11.5.2 Leaving a Legacy
- Consider the legacy you want to leave in your industry, community, and the world as you embark on new ventures and challenges.

Exiting a venture-backed startup is not the end of your entrepreneurial journey but the beginning of a new chapter filled with opportunities for personal and professional growth. By reflecting on your journey, considering various paths, and staying true to your goals and values, you can continue to make a meaningful impact on the entrepreneurial ecosystem and beyond. Congratulations on your achievements, and may your future endeavors be as fulfilling and successful as your past ones.

12

The Ever-Evolving Entrepreneurial Landscape

The entrepreneurial landscape is constantly evolving, driven by technological advancements, shifting market dynamics, and changing global trends. In this final chapter, we will explore the ever-changing nature of entrepreneurship and the key factors that entrepreneurs should keep in mind as they navigate this dynamic environment.

12.1 Technological Advancements

12.1.1 Tech Innovation
 - Stay informed about technological innovations that can impact your industry and create new opportunities.

12.1.2 Digital Transformation
 - Embrace digital transformation to streamline operations, enhance customer experiences, and remain competitive.

12.2 Market Trends

12.2.1 Market Research
- Continuously conduct market research to identify emerging trends, customer preferences, and market gaps.

12.2.2 Agile Business Models
- Develop agile business models that allow you to adapt quickly to changing market conditions.

12.3 Globalization and International Expansion

12.3.1 Global Opportunities
- Explore global markets for expansion and consider the implications of international operations.

12.3.2 Cross-Cultural Understanding
- Develop cross-cultural understanding and adapt your strategies to diverse markets and customer bases.

12.4 Sustainability and Social Responsibility

12.4.1 Environmental Responsibility
- Consider sustainability and environmental responsibility in your business practices to meet the expectations of modern consumers.

12.4.2 Social Impact
- Explore ways to make a positive social impact through your business, as social responsibility becomes a driving force in entrepreneurship.

12.5 Regulatory Changes

12.5.1 Regulatory Compliance
- Stay informed about evolving regulations and compliance requirements that affect your industry and business operations.

12.5.2 Legal Counsel
- Engage legal counsel to navigate complex regulatory changes and ensure your business remains compliant.

12.6 Collaboration and Partnerships

12.6.1 Ecosystem Engagement
- Participate in industry ecosystems, partnerships, and collaborations that can offer new opportunities and resources.

12.6.2 Open Innovation
- Embrace open innovation by collaborating with startups, accelerators, and other players in your industry to foster creativity and growth.

12.7 Lifelong Learning and Adaptability

12.7.1 Continuous Learning
- Commit to lifelong learning, acquiring new skills, and staying adaptable in the face of change.

12.7.2 Resilience
- Cultivate resilience to navigate challenges and setbacks that are an inherent part of the entrepreneurial journey.

The entrepreneurial landscape will continue to evolve, presenting both challenges and opportunities for those willing to embrace change and stay agile. As an entrepreneur, your ability to adapt, innovate, and align with emerging trends will be key to your long-term success. Keep an eye on the horizon, stay committed to your vision, and be prepared for the exciting journey ahead in the ever-evolving world of entrepreneurship.

13

Summary

The "Venture Capital Handbook for Entrepreneurs" is a comprehensive guide that explores the entrepreneurial journey from securing venture capital funding to the ever-evolving entrepreneurial landscape. It covers a wide range of topics in its 12 chapters:

1. Chapter 1 introduces the concept of venture capital and its importance for entrepreneurs.
2. Chapter 2 discusses the process of preparing for venture capital investment, including business planning and due diligence.
3. Chapter 3 focuses on the pitch and presentation to potential investors.
4. Chapter 4 delves into the negotiation process and the terms of a venture capital deal.
5. Chapter 5 explores the nuances of negotiating venture capital terms, including investment amount, equity ownership, and exit strategies.
6. Chapter 6 provides guidance on scaling a startup with venture capital funding.
7. Chapter 7 emphasizes the importance of managing the investor relationship effectively.
8. Chapter 8 addresses common challenges faced by venture-backed startups and strategies to overcome them.

9. Chapter 9 highlights the significance of achieving significant milestones and scaling a startup.
10. Chapter 10 covers the processes and considerations for successful exits, whether through acquisition or an IPO.
11. Chapter 11 discusses the possibilities for entrepreneurs in their next chapter after exiting a startup.
12. Chapter 12 concludes the guide by examining the ever-evolving entrepreneurial landscape, emphasizing the importance of adaptability and staying informed about technological advancements, market trends, globalization, sustainability, and regulatory changes.

This handbook serves as a valuable resource for entrepreneurs seeking venture capital and provides insights into building and growing successful startups in an ever-changing business landscape.

www.ingramcontent.com/pod-product-compliance
Lightning Source LLC
LaVergne TN
LVHW012128070526
838202LV00056B/5924